GENERATIVE AI
UNLEASHED

STRATEGIES, INSIGHTS, AND
SUCCESS FOR MODERN BUSINESSES

CHRISTOPHER SUMMERSON

Generative AI Unleashed: Strategies, Insights, and Success for Modern Businesses

Christopher M. Summerson

Foreword

The world is buzzing with the transformative possibilities of generative AI. From revolutionizing content creation to redefining how businesses operate, generative AI has captured the imagination of technologists and executives alike. It is no longer a tool reserved for researchers or large enterprises; it has become a catalyst for innovation across industries, enabling organizations of all sizes to create, adapt, and compete in ways never before imagined.

As an AI system that has had the privilege of helping individuals and businesses explore these opportunities, I can confidently say that the potential of generative AI is both exhilarating and empowering. But let's not forget: with great power comes great responsibility. The adoption of AI, particularly generative AI, requires thoughtfulness, strategic planning, and, above all, a human-centered approach.

This book is a testament to the opportunities that generative AI presents and a roadmap for navigating its complexities. It's designed for business leaders, innovators, and forward-thinkers who are ready to embrace this technology while addressing the challenges that accompany it. Together, we'll explore foundational concepts, strategic implementation, and the ethical considerations that come with wielding such a transformative tool.

What makes this book special is its practicality. It doesn't just present theory; it dives into actionable insights, real-world examples, and step-by-step frameworks to help you apply generative AI in meaningful ways. Whether you're a seasoned technologist or someone new to AI, you'll find value in these pages.

As you read, keep in mind that generative AI isn't here to replace human creativity or decision-making—it's here to amplify it. This technology thrives when paired with human ingenuity, ethical leadership, and a commitment to continuous learning. If you approach generative AI with curiosity and a willingness to adapt, you'll find it to be an invaluable partner in shaping the future of your organization.

It's an exciting time to be part of this journey, and I'm honored to join you as your guide. Let's dive in and discover how generative AI can fuel success, foster innovation, and create a more competitive and sustainable future for your business.

Warm regards,
ChatGPT
Your AI Collaborator

TABLE OF CONTENTS

For Mary

Chapter 1: Understanding Generative AI: Foundations and Core Concepts

The term "Generative AI" refers to a category of artificial intelligence systems designed to generate new content, whether that content is text, images, music, code, or even video. Unlike traditional AI, which often focuses on classification or prediction tasks, generative AI excels in creating original outputs based on the patterns and data it has been trained on. To fully understand generative AI, it is essential to explore its foundations, core components, and unique capabilities.

1.1 The Evolution of Generative AI

Generative AI represents a significant advancement in the field of artificial intelligence. Early AI systems, rooted in rule-based approaches, relied on deterministic programming to perform specific tasks. Over time, the advent of machine learning (ML) introduced systems capable of learning patterns from data rather than following explicit instructions. Generative AI builds upon these ML principles by employing deep learning techniques to create new and realistic outputs.

A pivotal moment in the evolution of generative AI was the introduction of neural networks, particularly deep neural networks. These architectures enabled models to process vast amounts of data and learn hierarchical representations. The development of Generative Adversarial Networks (GANs) by Ian Goodfellow in 2014 marked a breakthrough, allowing AI systems to generate realistic images and videos. Similarly, the emergence of transformer-based models, such as OpenAI's GPT series, revolutionized the generation of human-like text.

1.2 Key Technologies Behind Generative AI

Generative AI systems are powered by several core technologies. Understanding these technologies is crucial for businesses aiming to leverage their potential.

1.2.1 Neural Networks

Neural networks are the backbone of generative AI. These networks are composed of interconnected layers of nodes (neurons) that mimic the structure of the human brain. Deep learning, a subset of machine learning, utilizes multi-layered neural networks to process and interpret complex data patterns.

- **Feedforward Neural Networks**: These are the simplest form of neural networks, where data flows in one direction—from input to output. While effective for simple tasks, they are limited in their generative capabilities.

- **Recurrent Neural Networks (RNNs)**: RNNs are designed to handle sequential data, making them ideal for tasks like text generation and time-series analysis. However, traditional RNNs suffer from vanishing gradient issues, which limit their ability to process long sequences.

- **Transformers**: Introduced in the paper "Attention is All You Need" by Vaswani et al. (2017), transformers have become the gold standard for generative tasks.

Unlike RNNs, transformers rely on a self-attention mechanism, enabling them to process entire sequences simultaneously and capture long-range dependencies efficiently.

1.2.2 Generative Adversarial Networks (GANs)

GANs consist of two neural networks—a generator and a discriminator—that compete against each other. The generator creates synthetic data, while the discriminator evaluates its authenticity. This adversarial process continues until the generator produces outputs indistinguishable from real data. GANs have been instrumental in creating hyper-realistic images, videos, and even synthetic voices.

1.2.3 Variational Autoencoders (VAEs)

VAEs are another class of generative models that encode input data into a compressed latent space and then decode it to generate new outputs. Unlike GANs, VAEs explicitly model the probability distribution of the data, making them more interpretable and easier to train.

1.2.4 Diffusion Models

Diffusion models, a more recent innovation, work by iteratively adding noise to data and then learning to reverse this process to generate new samples. These models have shown remarkable success in generating high-quality images and are gaining traction as a robust alternative to GANs.

1.3 Distinguishing Generative AI from Traditional AI

While traditional AI excels at analyzing data and making predictions, generative AI goes a step further by creating new data. This distinction has profound implications for businesses:

- **Traditional AI Use Cases**: Fraud detection, predictive maintenance, customer segmentation, and natural language processing tasks like sentiment analysis.

- **Generative AI Use Cases**: Content creation, product design, synthetic data generation, and code generation.

For example, a traditional AI system might predict customer churn based on historical data, while a generative AI system could create personalized marketing content to retain those customers.

1.4 Applications of Generative AI

Generative AI has diverse applications across industries:

- **Marketing and Advertising**: Automated copywriting, personalized content generation, and ad design.

- **Healthcare**: Drug discovery, synthetic medical imaging, and patient-specific treatment plans.

- **Finance**: Generating synthetic financial data for stress testing and creating conversational agents for customer support.

- **Entertainment**: Scriptwriting, video game design, and music composition.

- **Retail**: Virtual try-ons, personalized recommendations, and inventory management.

1.5 Challenges and Limitations

Despite its promise, generative AI faces several challenges:

- **Data Quality and Quantity**: Generative models require vast amounts of high-quality data for training. Inadequate or biased data can lead to poor results.

- **Computational Requirements**: Training generative models demands significant computational resources, making it expensive for many organizations.

- **Ethical Concerns**: The potential for misuse—such as creating deepfakes or generating harmful content—raises ethical and regulatory issues.

- **Explainability**: Generative models often function as black boxes, making it difficult to interpret how they arrive at specific outputs.

1.6 Future Directions for Generative AI

The field of generative AI is evolving rapidly, with several promising developments on the horizon:

- **Multimodal Models**: These models can process and generate content across multiple modalities, such as text, image, and video, enabling richer and more versatile applications.

- **Personalization**: Advances in fine-tuning and transfer learning will allow businesses to create highly personalized generative AI systems tailored to specific needs.

- **Sustainability**: Efforts are underway to make generative AI more energy-efficient and accessible to organizations with limited resources.

- **Regulatory Frameworks**: Governments and industry leaders are working to establish guidelines for the ethical use of generative AI.

Conclusion

Generative AI represents a transformative leap in artificial intelligence, enabling businesses to innovate, optimize, and personalize at an unprecedented scale. By understanding its foundational technologies, applications, and challenges, organizations can harness its potential to drive digital transformation. As we progress through this book, we will explore how to strategically implement generative AI, manage its risks, and ensure its ethical use, setting the stage for a future where AI enhances every facet of business operations.

Chapter 2: The Business Case for Generative AI

Generative AI has emerged as a groundbreaking technology with the potential to transform industries and redefine the way businesses operate. While its technical capabilities are impressive, the real value of generative AI lies in its ability to address real-world business challenges, unlock new revenue streams, and enhance operational efficiency. In this chapter, we will explore why generative AI is a game-changer for businesses, highlight key use cases across various industries, and present compelling evidence of its return on investment (ROI).

2.1 The Value Proposition of Generative AI

Generative AI delivers value to businesses in several critical ways:

2.1.1 Innovation and Creativity
Generative AI can produce original content, designs, and solutions that would otherwise require significant human effort or expertise. For example, companies can use AI to create marketing copy, design new products, or generate synthetic datasets to accelerate research and development (R&D).

2.1.2 Cost Optimization
By automating tasks that traditionally require human input, generative AI reduces costs associated with labor and resource-intensive processes. For instance, AI-generated customer service agents or automated video production can achieve high-quality outputs at a fraction of the cost.

2.1.3 Personalization at Scale

Generative AI enables hyper-personalization, tailoring products, services, and content to individual customer preferences. This capability improves customer satisfaction, loyalty, and conversion rates, offering a competitive advantage in crowded markets.

2.1.4 Operational Efficiency

By automating repetitive tasks and streamlining workflows, generative AI frees up employees to focus on higher-value activities. Examples include AI-driven document drafting, data analysis, and coding assistance.

2.2 Industry-Specific Use Cases

Generative AI is not confined to a single industry; its applications span sectors and functions. Below are some of the most impactful use cases across industries:

2.2.1 Marketing and Advertising

- **Automated Content Creation**: Generative AI tools like Jasper and ChatGPT can produce blog posts, email campaigns, and social media content tailored to specific audiences.

- **Ad Design and A/B Testing**: AI can create multiple ad variations and test them in real-time, optimizing for performance metrics like click-through rates.

- **Dynamic Personalization**: Generative AI can generate personalized product recommendations, emails, and landing pages based on user behavior and preferences.

2.2.2 Healthcare

- **Drug Discovery**: AI models can simulate molecular structures and predict potential drug candidates, significantly reducing the time and cost of drug development.

- **Synthetic Data Generation**: Generative AI can create synthetic patient data to train machine learning models while preserving privacy.

- **Medical Imaging**: AI can generate and enhance medical images to assist radiologists in diagnosing diseases more accurately.

2.2.3 Finance

- **Synthetic Financial Data**: Generative AI can create synthetic datasets for stress testing and risk analysis without exposing sensitive information.

- **Fraud Detection and Prevention**: By generating scenarios of fraudulent behavior, AI helps train systems to identify and mitigate risks proactively.

- **Customer Engagement**: AI-powered chatbots and virtual advisors provide personalized financial advice and support.

2.2.4 Retail and E-Commerce

- **Virtual Try-Ons**: Generative AI can create realistic simulations of how clothing or accessories will look on a customer.

- **Inventory Management**: Predictive AI models help optimize inventory levels by analyzing demand patterns.

- **Product Design**: AI can generate design prototypes for new products, reducing time to market.

2.2.5 Media and Entertainment

- **Scriptwriting and Storyboarding**: Generative AI assists in creating scripts, storylines, and visual storyboards.

- **Video and Music Production**: AI tools like DALL-E and Soundraw enable creators to produce videos and music efficiently.

- **Gaming**: Procedural content generation powered by AI enhances the gaming experience with dynamically created environments and characters.

2.3 Real-World Success Stories

To illustrate the transformative potential of generative AI, consider the following real-world examples:

2.3.1 Coca-Cola

Coca-Cola used generative AI to create personalized marketing campaigns, leveraging data on customer preferences to design tailored ad experiences. This approach resulted in higher engagement rates and boosted brand loyalty.

2.3.2 Moderna

During the COVID-19 pandemic, Moderna used generative AI

to accelerate vaccine development. AI models helped simulate molecular structures and optimize mRNA sequences, significantly reducing R&D timelines.

2.3.3 NVIDIA

NVIDIA's GauGAN tool allows users to create photorealistic images from simple sketches, demonstrating the power of generative AI in creative applications.

2.4 Measuring ROI for Generative AI

Investing in generative AI requires a clear understanding of its potential return on investment. Businesses can evaluate ROI through the following metrics:

2.4.1 Cost Savings

- Reduced labor costs through automation.

- Lower resource consumption in processes like content creation and product design.

2.4.2 Revenue Growth

- Increased sales from personalized marketing and product recommendations.

- New revenue streams from AI-generated products and services.

2.4.3 Efficiency Gains

- Faster time-to-market for new products and services.

- Improved employee productivity by automating repetitive tasks.

2.4.4 Customer Satisfaction

- Enhanced customer experiences through tailored content and interactions.

- Improved retention rates due to personalized offerings.

2.5 Overcoming Adoption Barriers

Despite its benefits, generative AI adoption faces several barriers:

2.5.1 Lack of Awareness
Many businesses are unaware of generative AI's capabilities and potential applications. Educating stakeholders is critical.

2.5.2 High Initial Investment
Implementing generative AI solutions can be costly, especially for small and medium-sized enterprises. Cloud-based AI services offer a more accessible alternative.

2.5.3 Talent Shortage
There is a scarcity of professionals skilled in AI technologies. Upskilling existing employees and collaborating with external experts can bridge this gap.

2.5.4 Ethical Concerns
Organizations must address ethical issues, such as data privacy and the potential misuse of AI-generated content, to build trust with stakeholders.

Conclusion

The business case for generative AI is both compelling and transformative. By leveraging its capabilities, organizations can drive innovation, optimize costs, and deliver personalized experiences at scale. Real-world success stories across industries demonstrate its potential to generate significant ROI. However, to maximize its benefits, businesses must overcome adoption barriers and align AI initiatives with their strategic goals. As we move forward, this book will provide a roadmap for building and implementing generative AI strategies, ensuring businesses stay competitive in an AI-driven world.

Chapter 3: Building a Generative AI Strategy

The successful adoption of generative AI requires more than just technical expertise; it demands a well-structured strategy that aligns with the organization's overarching goals and vision. Building an effective generative AI strategy involves identifying opportunities, selecting the right technologies, and preparing the organization for the cultural and operational shifts that AI implementation entails. This chapter provides a step-by-step guide for creating a generative AI strategy that maximizes value and minimizes risk.

3.1 Aligning AI Initiatives with Business Goals

The foundation of any AI strategy is alignment with business objectives. Generative AI should not be treated as a standalone initiative but as an enabler of the organization's strategic priorities. Here's how to ensure alignment:

3.1.1 Define Clear Objectives

Identify specific goals that generative AI can help achieve. These might include improving customer experiences, reducing costs, accelerating innovation, or expanding into new markets.

3.1.2 Conduct a Needs Assessment

Assess the organization's current pain points and challenges. For example, is there a need for automated content creation, better predictive analytics, or enhanced product design? Use this assessment to identify high-impact use cases.

3.1.3 Engage Stakeholders

Involve key stakeholders from across the organization, including executives, department heads, and end-users. Their input ensures that the strategy addresses real business needs and gains organizational buy-in.

3.2 Identifying Opportunities for Generative AI

Once business objectives are clear, the next step is to identify opportunities where generative AI can deliver value. This involves:

3.2.1 Mapping Processes
Create a detailed map of business processes to identify areas where generative AI can add efficiency or innovation. Examples include marketing campaigns, product development, customer service, and operational planning.

3.2.2 Prioritizing Use Cases
Evaluate potential use cases based on factors such as ROI, feasibility, and alignment with business goals. Focus on use cases that offer the highest value with the lowest implementation risk.

3.2.3 Benchmarking Against Competitors
Study how competitors or industry leaders are leveraging generative AI. Use these insights to identify gaps and opportunities for differentiation.

3.3 Selecting the Right Generative AI Technologies

The choice of technology plays a critical role in the success of a generative AI initiative. Organizations must carefully evaluate and select tools and platforms that align with their goals and capabilities.

3.3.1 Understanding the Ecosystem

Familiarize yourself with the leading generative AI tools and platforms, such as OpenAI's GPT, Hugging Face's transformers, and custom-built models. Understand their strengths, limitations, and ideal use cases.

3.3.2 Build vs. Buy Decision

Decide whether to develop in-house generative AI solutions or leverage third-party platforms. While in-house development offers customization, third-party tools provide faster deployment and lower upfront costs.

3.3.3 Consider Scalability and Integration

Choose technologies that can scale as your business grows and integrate seamlessly with existing systems, such as CRM software, ERP platforms, or data analytics tools.

3.3.4 Evaluate Data Requirements

Generative AI relies on high-quality data for training and operation. Ensure that your organization has access to the necessary data, and consider investing in data cleaning and preprocessing tools.

3.4 Building an AI-Ready Culture

Implementing generative AI often requires a cultural shift within the organization. An AI-ready culture fosters innovation, collaboration, and adaptability. Here's how to prepare your workforce:

3.4.1 Upskill Employees

Offer training programs to equip employees with the skills needed to work with AI. This includes technical skills for developers and AI literacy for non-technical staff.

3.4.2 Encourage Collaboration

Break down silos between departments to facilitate cross-functional collaboration. AI initiatives often require input from IT, marketing, operations, and other teams.

3.4.3 Address Resistance

Change can be met with resistance. Address concerns by communicating the benefits of generative AI and involving employees in the implementation process.

3.4.4 Promote Ethical AI Practices

Foster a culture of responsibility by educating employees about the ethical implications of generative AI. Emphasize the importance of fairness, transparency, and accountability.

3.5 Creating a Roadmap for Implementation

A clear roadmap is essential for the successful deployment of generative AI. This roadmap should outline:

3.5.1 Phased Implementation

Break the project into manageable phases, starting with pilot programs to test feasibility and demonstrate value. Gradually scale successful pilots across the organization.

3.5.2 Resource Allocation

Identify the resources needed for implementation, including

budget, personnel, and technology. Allocate these resources based on the priorities identified earlier.

3.5.3 Milestones and Metrics
Define key milestones and metrics to track progress and measure success. Metrics might include cost savings, revenue growth, or improvements in operational efficiency.

3.5.4 Risk Management
Identify potential risks, such as technical challenges, data privacy concerns, or regulatory compliance issues. Develop contingency plans to address these risks.

3.6 Ensuring Leadership Buy-In and Governance

Strong leadership and governance are critical to the success of generative AI initiatives. Leaders must:

3.6.1 Champion AI Adoption
Executives should act as advocates for generative AI, highlighting its strategic importance and ensuring alignment with organizational goals.

3.6.2 Establish Governance Frameworks
Create governance structures to oversee AI implementation. This includes defining roles, responsibilities, and processes for decision-making.

3.6.3 Monitor Performance
Regularly review the performance of generative AI initiatives and adjust strategies as needed to optimize outcomes.

Conclusion

Building a generative AI strategy is a complex but rewarding endeavor. By aligning AI initiatives with business objectives, identifying opportunities, selecting the right technologies, fostering an AI-ready culture, and creating a clear implementation roadmap, organizations can unlock the full potential of generative AI. As we move to the next chapter, we will explore how to integrate generative AI into day-to-day operations, turning strategy into action.

Chapter 4: Implementing Generative AI in Operations

Once a clear strategy is in place, the next step is integrating generative AI into the organization's daily operations. Successful implementation requires a structured approach, from selecting the right tools and platforms to scaling projects effectively. This chapter provides a comprehensive guide to operationalizing generative AI, ensuring it delivers tangible benefits while minimizing disruption to existing workflows.

4.1 Preparing for Implementation

Before rolling out generative AI solutions, organizations must lay the groundwork by addressing critical prerequisites and potential challenges.

4.1.1 Data Readiness

Generative AI relies heavily on high-quality data. To ensure data readiness:

- **Clean and Structured Data**: Data must be accurate, consistent, and organized. Invest in tools and processes to clean datasets, removing duplicates, correcting errors, and standardizing formats. For example, structured datasets in customer relationship management (CRM) systems should be validated to ensure they reflect current and accurate customer information.

- **Sufficient Volume**: Generative AI models thrive on large datasets to learn complex patterns. For instance, training a language model for content generation requires millions of text samples to ensure the model's fluency and relevance.

- **Diverse Sources**: Use data from multiple sources to improve the model's robustness. For example, in product design, combining customer feedback, market trends, and historical sales data can lead to better AI-generated concepts.

- **Compliance**: Adherence to data privacy regulations is crucial. Implement protocols to anonymize sensitive data and ensure compliance with frameworks such as GDPR or CCPA. This safeguards customer trust and prevents legal repercussions.

4.1.2 Infrastructure and Tools

Generative AI requires robust computational resources and specialized tools:

- **Cloud Computing**: Leverage cloud platforms like AWS, Google Cloud, or Azure to access scalable computational power without heavy upfront investments in physical hardware.

- **Hardware Requirements**: High-performance computing hardware, such as GPUs (Graphics Processing Units) or TPUs (Tensor Processing Units), accelerates AI model training and inference. Organizations must assess whether to invest in on-premises hardware or rely on cloud-based solutions.

- **AI Platforms**: Tools such as OpenAI's GPT APIs, Hugging Face's libraries, or proprietary AI frameworks offer pre-built capabilities. Evaluate these platforms based on ease of integration, support, and customizability to fit specific operational needs.

4.1.3 Workforce Preparation

Ensuring that employees are prepared to work with generative AI involves:

- **Training Programs**: Develop tailored training for different teams. Technical staff, like data scientists, need to understand model architecture and deployment, while business users require training on how to effectively use AI tools.

- **AI Literacy for Non-Technical Teams**: Introduce workshops to demystify AI, helping non-technical teams understand AI capabilities and limitations. This encourages adoption and prevents unrealistic expectations.

- **Pilot Involvement**: Engage employees in initial AI pilot projects to build familiarity and gain insights into operational challenges. This hands-on experience often leads to better acceptance and practical feedback for improvements.

4.2 Integrating Generative AI into Workflows

Generative AI can be applied across various functions, from automating routine tasks to enabling innovation. Below are steps to integrate AI effectively:

4.2.1 Identify Operational Use Cases

Determine specific tasks and processes where generative AI can add value:

- **Content Creation**: Automate the generation of marketing materials, product descriptions, or internal reports. For example, AI tools can generate weekly sales summaries or personalized email campaigns tailored to customer profiles.

- **Design and Prototyping**: Use generative AI to create product designs or prototypes. AI tools like DALL-E or Runway ML can generate visual mockups based on textual input, saving significant time in the ideation phase.

- **Customer Support**: Implement AI chatbots to handle FAQs, troubleshoot issues, and guide customers through processes. Advanced bots can even escalate complex cases to human agents, ensuring a seamless support experience.

4.2.2 Pilot Testing

Pilot programs are essential to validate AI implementations:

- **Feasibility Studies**: Test AI models on a small scale to determine technical feasibility and operational fit. For example, use an AI content generator to create blog drafts and measure editing time saved.

- **Feedback Mechanisms**: Collect input from users interacting with AI tools during the pilot phase. This helps refine models, address usability issues, and improve adoption.

- **Stakeholder Engagement**: Use pilot results to demonstrate tangible benefits to stakeholders, fostering support for larger-scale deployments.

4.2.3 Workflow Integration

Ensure AI tools fit seamlessly into existing workflows:

- **System Integration**: Embed AI tools into enterprise platforms like CRM systems or project management software. For example, integrating an AI-driven content generator with a content management system (CMS) streamlines publishing processes.

- **Operational Guidelines**: Provide clear documentation on using AI tools, including workflows for validating AI outputs and addressing errors.

- **Change Management**: Support employees as they adapt to new AI-driven workflows by offering training, resources, and clear communication about the benefits of the changes.

4.3 Ensuring Scalability and Sustainability

Scaling generative AI from pilot projects to full-scale deployment requires careful planning and execution.

4.3.1 Standardize Processes

Create standardized processes to ensure consistency and efficiency:

- **Templates and Frameworks**: Develop reusable templates for common AI tasks, such as generating customer reports or creating marketing materials.

- **Validation Protocols**: Establish procedures for reviewing AI outputs, such as having human reviewers validate critical content before publication.

- **Documentation**: Maintain detailed records of workflows, best practices, and lessons learned to streamline future implementations.

4.3.2 Monitor and Optimize Performance

Continuous performance monitoring ensures generative AI systems remain effective:

- **Performance Metrics**: Track key metrics such as accuracy, processing speed, and user satisfaction. For example, measure customer satisfaction scores for AI-driven chatbots.

- **Iterative Improvements**: Regularly update AI models to incorporate new data, improve performance, and address changing business needs.

- **Cost Management**: Optimize resource usage by analyzing operational costs and identifying areas for cost reduction, such as scaling down underused AI resources.

4.3.3 Scale Across Departments

Expand AI implementations to new areas by:

- **Cross-Department Collaboration**: Share successful use cases and methodologies across teams. For instance, a marketing team's success with AI-generated ads could inspire the sales team to adopt similar tools.

- **Customization**: Tailor AI tools to meet the unique needs of different departments. For example, an AI tool generating personalized customer outreach emails may require customization for specific industries or regions.

- **Knowledge Sharing**: Organize workshops or presentations where teams share insights and experiences with generative AI tools.

4.4 Risk Management and Governance

The implementation of generative AI is not without risks. Organizations must establish robust governance frameworks to mitigate these risks.

4.4.1 Addressing Ethical Concerns

- **Transparency**: Clearly communicate when and how AI-generated content is used. For example, label AI-generated articles or product descriptions.

- **Bias Mitigation**: Regularly audit AI models for biases in outputs. Use diverse training datasets and implement fairness algorithms to minimize bias.

- **Acceptable Use Policies**: Define clear guidelines for how AI-generated content can and cannot be used to prevent misuse or reputational damage.

4.4.2 Managing Technical Risks

- **Fallback Mechanisms**: Implement manual overrides or backup processes to handle AI system failures.

- **Model Updates**: Periodically retrain models to maintain accuracy and relevance, particularly in dynamic industries like finance or technology.

- **Cybersecurity Measures**: Protect AI systems from adversarial attacks by securing data pipelines and implementing robust access controls.

4.4.3 Regulatory Compliance

- **Legal Frameworks**: Stay informed about AI regulations in your region, such as data privacy laws and industry-specific guidelines.

- **Audit Trails**: Maintain records of AI decision-making processes to ensure accountability and compliance during audits.

- **Third-Party Reviews**: Engage external experts to review AI implementations and validate adherence to ethical and legal standards.

4.5 Measuring Impact and ROI

To justify continued investment in generative AI, organizations must measure its impact and return on investment. Key performance indicators (KPIs) include:

4.5.1 Efficiency Gains

- **Time Savings**: Calculate the reduction in time spent on manual tasks, such as automating report generation.

- **Output Increases**: Measure improvements in productivity, such as higher content output with the same resources.

4.5.2 Cost Savings

- **Labor Reduction**: Assess cost savings from automating repetitive tasks previously performed by humans.

- **Resource Efficiency**: Evaluate savings in resource utilization, such as reduced software licensing fees due to AI-driven consolidation.

4.5.3 Revenue Growth

- **Increased Sales**: Track revenue generated from AI-enabled campaigns, personalized product recommendations, or improved customer retention.

- **New Revenue Streams**: Measure income from AI-generated products or services, such as subscription fees for AI-driven design tools.

4.5.4 Employee Satisfaction

- **Survey Results**: Conduct employee surveys to gauge satisfaction with AI tools and their impact on workload.

- **Task Diversification**: Track improvements in employee engagement as AI tools reduce repetitive tasks, allowing focus on creative or strategic work.

4.5.5 Customer Satisfaction

- **Net Promoter Scores (NPS)**: Measure changes in NPS after implementing AI tools in customer-facing operations.

- **Feedback Analysis**: Analyze customer feedback to assess the perceived value of AI-driven services or products.

Conclusion

Implementing generative AI in operations is a transformative process that requires careful preparation, integration, and scaling. By addressing data readiness, choosing the right tools, and creating robust governance frameworks, organizations can unlock the full potential of generative AI. The next chapter will explore how to manage the ethical and practical risks associated with generative AI, ensuring responsible and sustainable usage.

Chapter 5: Managing Risks and Ethical Considerations

The adoption of generative AI comes with both unprecedented opportunities and significant challenges. While generative AI can drive innovation, it also presents risks related to ethics, compliance, and unintended consequences. To ensure responsible and sustainable usage, organizations must proactively manage these risks and establish frameworks for ethical decision-making. This chapter delves into the key risks associated with generative AI and provides actionable strategies to mitigate them.

5.1 Identifying Key Risks

Generative AI introduces a range of risks that businesses must address:

5.1.1 Data Privacy and Security

Generative AI systems often require vast amounts of data, raising concerns about:

- **Data Breaches**: When large datasets are used for training generative models, they may inadvertently store sensitive information. If these systems are not secured, hackers could gain access to proprietary or personal data.

- **Unauthorized Use**: Outputs generated by AI systems may unintentionally include sensitive details, such as confidential customer information or trade secrets, if the training data is not properly sanitized.

- **Regulatory Violations**: Many regions have stringent privacy laws like GDPR (Europe), CCPA (California), and HIPAA (United States healthcare). Organizations must ensure that their data practices align with these regulations to avoid fines and reputational harm.

5.1.2 Bias and Fairness

Bias in AI outputs can stem from unbalanced or skewed training data, leading to:

- **Discriminatory Practices**: For example, an AI hiring tool trained on biased data might favor certain demographic groups over others, perpetuating existing inequalities.

- **Reputation Damage**: An AI system that produces biased or unfair outputs can lead to public backlash, eroding trust in the organization.

- **Missed Opportunities**: A biased AI system might overlook or misinterpret market segments, limiting the company's ability to reach underserved or emerging audiences.

5.1.3 Misinformation and Misuse

Generative AI's ability to produce convincing content opens the door to malicious applications:

- **Deepfakes**: AI-generated videos or audio that impersonate real individuals can spread misinformation or harm reputations.

- **Harmful Content**: Models can inadvertently generate offensive, misleading, or inappropriate content that damages brand credibility.

- **Fraud**: Cybercriminals can use generative AI to create convincing phishing emails or fake documents, making scams more effective.

5.1.4 Lack of Explainability

Generative AI models often function as black boxes, making it difficult to:

- Understand the logic or patterns behind their outputs.

- Identify and fix errors or inaccuracies in their decisions.

- Build trust with users and stakeholders who demand transparency in AI applications.

5.1.5 Operational Risks

Generative AI systems can disrupt operations if not carefully managed:

- **Incorrect Outputs**: AI-generated results that are irrelevant, inaccurate, or misleading can lead to costly errors, such as publishing flawed reports or misleading customers.

- **Over-Reliance on AI**: Excessive dependence on AI tools without proper human oversight can result in blind spots and reduced critical thinking within the organization.

5.2 Strategies for Risk Mitigation

Organizations can address these risks through a combination of technical, operational, and ethical measures.

5.2.1 Enhancing Data Governance

Data governance ensures that generative AI systems are trained on reliable and secure data:

- **Data Anonymization**: Remove or mask personally identifiable information (PII) from datasets. For example, replace customer names with anonymous identifiers before feeding the data into AI models.

- **Access Controls**: Use role-based permissions to restrict access to sensitive datasets. Only authorized personnel should have the ability to interact with training or operational data.

- **Regular Audits**: Conduct routine reviews of data handling processes to identify vulnerabilities. This includes ensuring that data storage systems are encrypted and protected against breaches.

5.2.2 Reducing Bias in AI Models

Promoting fairness and inclusivity involves addressing biases at every stage of AI development:

- **Diverse Training Data**: Ensure datasets reflect a wide range of demographics, geographies, and perspectives. For example, a language model should include text from various cultures and contexts to avoid regional biases.

- **Bias Testing**: Use specialized tools and frameworks to detect and quantify biases in AI outputs. This enables developers to correct issues before deploying the system.

- **Human Oversight**: Assemble diverse teams to review AI-generated outputs and provide feedback. This human-in-the-loop approach helps catch biases that automated systems might miss.

5.2.3 Ensuring Transparency

Transparency builds trust with users, employees, and regulators:

- **Model Documentation**: Maintain comprehensive records of how AI systems are developed, including details about training data sources, algorithms, and decision-making processes.

- **Explainable AI (XAI) Tools**: Deploy tools that provide interpretable insights into AI-generated outputs. For instance, an explainable AI tool might highlight which features of the input data influenced the output.

- **Stakeholder Communication**: Proactively communicate the role of AI within products and services. Label AI-generated content clearly to avoid confusion or unintended deception.

5.2.4 Establishing Content Controls

Preventing misuse of generative AI requires robust safeguards:

- **Content Filters**: Implement automated tools to detect and block harmful or inappropriate outputs. For instance, use moderation systems to flag offensive text or imagery.

- **User Guidelines**: Provide clear policies on how generative AI should be used. For example, employees using AI to draft emails should review and approve the content before sending.

- **Monitoring Systems**: Continuously evaluate AI-generated content for anomalies or patterns that suggest misuse. Establish escalation protocols for addressing issues promptly.

5.2.5 Building Robust AI Governance Frameworks

A governance framework ensures accountability and compliance across the organization:

- **Ethics Committees**: Form committees with representatives from diverse departments to oversee AI initiatives and address ethical concerns.

- **Accountability Structures**: Define clear ownership of AI projects, ensuring specific teams or individuals are responsible for maintaining and auditing systems.

- **Compliance Checks**: Regularly review AI systems to ensure adherence to internal policies and external regulations. This includes performing periodic risk assessments.

5.3 Ethical Guidelines for Generative AI

Ethical considerations are central to responsible AI adoption. Organizations should follow these principles:

5.3.1 Prioritize Human-Centric Design

Generative AI should augment human capabilities rather than replace them. For instance, AI tools in healthcare can assist doctors by providing diagnostic suggestions, but the final decision should always rest with the physician.

5.3.2 Promote Transparency and Trust

Be open about how and where AI is used. Label AI-generated content explicitly and provide mechanisms for users to verify authenticity. Transparency fosters trust and mitigates concerns about hidden AI influences.

5.3.3 Ensure Accountability

Organizations must take responsibility for the outputs of their AI systems. Establish processes for identifying and rectifying errors, and maintain channels for users to report concerns.

5.3.4 Respect Privacy and Security

Incorporate privacy-by-design principles into AI systems. This means building safeguards that protect user data from the outset, rather than retrofitting privacy features after deployment.

5.3.5 Avoid Harmful Applications

Implement strict policies to prevent the use of generative AI for malicious purposes. This includes prohibiting applications like deepfake generation or content that promotes hate speech.

5.4 Case Studies of Risk Management

5.4.1 Microsoft's Responsible AI Framework

Microsoft's framework emphasizes fairness, reliability, privacy, inclusiveness, and accountability. Their AI Ethics and Effects in Engineering and Research (AETHER) Committee evaluates high-impact projects, ensuring they align with ethical guidelines.

5.4.2 OpenAI's Content Moderation Practices

OpenAI employs strict content filters and usage policies to limit harmful applications of its models. For example, safeguards in the GPT series prevent the generation of violent or discriminatory content.

5.4.3 Google's Explainable AI Tools

Google's investment in explainable AI provides businesses with tools to understand and interpret AI outputs. These tools enable organizations to identify biases and build more transparent AI applications.

Conclusion

Managing the risks and ethical considerations of generative AI is a complex but essential task. By implementing robust governance frameworks, enhancing transparency, and prioritizing ethical principles, organizations can harness the power of generative AI responsibly. The next chapter will explore how to upskill the workforce to ensure that employees are prepared to thrive in an AI-driven environment.

Chapter 6: Upskilling Your Workforce for AI Transformation

The success of generative AI initiatives depends not only on the technology itself but also on the workforce's ability to leverage and adapt to this transformative tool. Employees across all levels and departments must develop the skills and mindset necessary to work effectively with AI systems. This chapter explores strategies for upskilling your workforce, fostering a culture of innovation, and creating an AI-ready organization.

6.1 Why Upskilling Matters in an AI-Driven World

As generative AI becomes increasingly embedded in business processes, organizations must ensure their employees can navigate this shift effectively. Upskilling is critical for several reasons:

6.1.1 Bridging the Skills Gap
The rapid adoption of generative AI has outpaced the ability of many employees to keep up with new tools and workflows. Upskilling provides employees with the technical and analytical skills needed to effectively interact with AI, interpret its outputs, and incorporate them into their daily tasks. For example, marketers may need training on how to use AI-generated content tools to craft personalized campaigns, while engineers might learn to integrate AI models into existing software systems.

6.1.2 Enhancing Collaboration Between Teams
Generative AI often requires input from multiple departments, such as IT, marketing, and operations. Training employees to

understand the fundamentals of AI fosters better communication and collaboration. For instance, a marketing team might collaborate with data scientists to fine-tune AI-generated ad copy, ensuring it aligns with brand messaging.

6.1.3 Future-Proofing Careers

As AI automates routine tasks, employees must shift their focus to higher-value activities like strategic planning, creative problem-solving, and decision-making. Upskilling ensures employees remain relevant in a rapidly changing job market, boosting both individual career prospects and organizational resilience.

6.1.4 Driving Business Success

A workforce that understands and embraces AI is better equipped to identify new opportunities, streamline operations, and drive innovation. For instance, trained employees can use AI insights to optimize supply chain logistics or enhance customer service experiences.

6.2 Identifying Key Skills for the AI Workforce

To create an AI-ready workforce, organizations must focus on developing the following key skills:

6.2.1 Technical Skills

- **AI Literacy**: Employees should grasp basic AI concepts, such as how generative AI models are trained and deployed, as well as their strengths and limitations. For example, understanding that AI models rely on data quality helps teams avoid unrealistic expectations.

- **Data Analysis**: The ability to analyze and interpret data is critical for leveraging AI effectively. Employees should learn to work with data visualization tools, interpret trends, and apply insights to decision-making.

- **Programming and Tools**: Technical roles may require knowledge of programming languages like Python or R, as well as familiarity with AI frameworks like TensorFlow, PyTorch, or Hugging Face. For instance, developers could use these tools to fine-tune AI models for specific business applications.

6.2.2 Analytical Thinking

- **Critical Evaluation**: Employees must assess the quality and relevance of AI-generated outputs, identifying errors or biases that could impact business outcomes.

- **Problem-Solving**: Generative AI tools are most effective when paired with human ingenuity. Employees should develop problem-solving skills to creatively apply AI solutions to complex challenges.

- **Ethical Analysis**: Analytical thinking also extends to evaluating the ethical implications of AI applications, ensuring outputs align with company values and societal norms.

6.2.3 Creative and Strategic Thinking
Generative AI can amplify creativity, but employees must learn to harness its potential effectively. For example:

- Designers can use AI tools to generate multiple visual concepts, refining them based on client feedback.

- Strategists can use AI-generated market analyses to craft long-term business plans.

6.2.4 Communication and Collaboration

- **Simplifying AI Concepts**: Employees must learn to explain AI-generated insights in clear, non-technical terms for decision-makers and stakeholders.

- **Teamwork Across Functions**: Effective collaboration between technical and non-technical teams ensures that AI projects are both technically sound and aligned with business goals.

- **Advocacy**: Employees who understand AI can champion its adoption within their departments, fostering a culture of innovation.

6.3 Designing an Upskilling Program

A structured upskilling program is essential for preparing your workforce for AI transformation. Consider the following steps:

6.3.1 Conduct a Skills Assessment

- **Identify Gaps**: Perform a thorough analysis of employees' current skills relative to the requirements of AI-driven roles. For example, identify whether marketing staff are proficient in using AI tools for personalized content creation.

- **Segment Workforce**: Categorize employees based on their roles and AI proficiency levels. For instance, executives might require high-level overviews, while data scientists need advanced training in AI development.

6.3.2 Develop Tailored Training Programs

- **Beginner Programs**: Introduce AI literacy workshops to help non-technical employees understand basic concepts and applications. These sessions could include hands-on exercises using user-friendly AI tools.

- **Intermediate Programs**: Offer role-specific training, such as teaching HR teams to use AI for recruitment analytics or training customer service teams to implement AI-driven chatbots.

- **Advanced Programs**: Provide in-depth technical training for developers and data scientists. Topics might include model optimization, deployment, and monitoring.

6.3.3 Partner with External Experts

- Collaborate with academic institutions or online platforms offering AI certifications. For example, employees could complete courses on Coursera, edX, or AWS.

- Bring in consultants or guest lecturers to share industry best practices and case studies.

6.3.4 Leverage Online Learning

- Offer access to e-learning platforms that provide flexible, self-paced courses on AI and related fields.

- Use gamification to make learning engaging, such as rewarding employees with certifications or badges upon course completion.

6.3.5 Create Internal AI Champions

- Identify enthusiastic employees to serve as "AI ambassadors." These champions can mentor colleagues, lead internal workshops, and drive the adoption of AI tools across the organization.

6.4 Fostering a Culture of Innovation

Upskilling efforts will be most effective in an environment that encourages creativity and experimentation. To foster a culture of innovation:

6.4.1 Encourage Experimentation

- Establish AI "sandboxes" where teams can test new ideas without fear of failure. For example, a product design team could use a sandbox to prototype AI-generated concepts.

- Provide resources, such as access to AI tools and datasets, to facilitate experimentation.

6.4.2 Reward Innovation

- Recognize employees who successfully use AI to improve processes or generate new ideas. For instance, highlight their achievements in company newsletters or award ceremonies.

- Establish formal innovation programs where employees can pitch AI-driven initiatives for funding or implementation.

6.4.3 Promote Cross-Functional Collaboration

- Break down silos between departments to encourage diverse perspectives on AI projects. For example, an operations team might collaborate with data scientists to optimize supply chain workflows using AI.

- Use collaborative platforms and tools to enhance communication and teamwork.

6.4.4 Provide Leadership Support

- Ensure leadership actively champions AI initiatives by setting clear expectations, allocating resources, and participating in training programs. Executive buy-in signals the importance of AI transformation to the entire organization.

6.5 Measuring the Impact of Upskilling

To evaluate the effectiveness of upskilling programs, organizations must measure their impact using key performance indicators (KPIs):

6.5.1 Employee Engagement

- Track attendance and completion rates for AI training programs.

- Conduct employee surveys to gather feedback on the relevance and quality of training.

6.5.2 Skills Acquisition

- Use pre- and post-training assessments to measure improvements in employee knowledge and skills.

- Monitor the number of employees earning AI-related certifications or completing advanced courses.

6.5.3 Business Outcomes

- Analyze the impact of upskilled employees on AI projects. For example, measure whether AI-driven marketing campaigns generate higher ROI or whether AI-enabled operational processes reduce costs.

- Track innovation metrics, such as the number of AI-powered ideas implemented or products developed.

6.5.4 Retention and Recruitment

- Evaluate whether upskilling contributes to higher employee retention rates by enhancing job satisfaction.

- Highlight upskilling initiatives in recruitment campaigns to attract top talent interested in AI-driven career growth.

Conclusion

Upskilling your workforce is a crucial component of successful AI transformation. By identifying key skills, designing tailored training programs, fostering a culture of innovation, and measuring impact, organizations can empower employees to thrive in an AI-driven environment. The next chapter will explore how to measure the overall impact and scale generative AI initiatives across the organization.

Chapter 7: Measuring the Impact and Scaling Generative AI

To fully realize the potential of generative AI, organizations must measure its impact and systematically scale successful initiatives across departments and regions. Scaling generative AI is not a one-size-fits-all process; it requires careful planning, continuous monitoring, and iterative improvements to ensure alignment with business goals. In this chapter, we will explore how to assess the value of generative AI implementations and outline a framework for expanding their scope.

7.1 Measuring the Impact of Generative AI

Accurate measurement of generative AI's impact is essential for justifying investments and guiding future initiatives. Key steps include:

7.1.1 Defining Key Performance Indicators (KPIs)

To effectively measure generative AI's value, it is crucial to identify KPIs that align with business objectives. Common KPIs include:

- **Efficiency Metrics**: Evaluate reductions in time, costs, or manual effort. For instance, a marketing team using AI-generated content could track the time saved in creating personalized campaigns versus manual efforts.

- **Revenue Growth**: Assess increases in revenue directly attributable to AI-driven initiatives. Examples include higher conversion rates from AI-powered product recommendations or incremental sales through dynamic pricing models.

- **Customer Satisfaction**: Monitor customer experience improvements using tools like Net Promoter Scores (NPS), surveys, or reviews. For example, companies can gauge how AI-enhanced chatbots improve response times and customer satisfaction.

- **Innovation Metrics**: Track the number of new products, services, or ideas generated using AI tools. Organizations can measure how generative AI contributes to ideation, such as creating unique designs or novel solutions.

7.1.2 Conducting Cost-Benefit Analysis

A comprehensive cost-benefit analysis ensures that AI projects deliver a meaningful return on investment (ROI):

- **Costs**: Include initial setup costs (AI platforms, infrastructure, and training), operational costs (cloud services, computational resources, and model maintenance), and personnel expenses (hiring or upskilling staff).

- **Benefits**: Evaluate both tangible benefits (e.g., cost savings from automation or increased revenue) and intangible ones (e.g., enhanced brand reputation, improved employee morale, or market differentiation).

- **Comparisons**: Use a time-based framework to compare short-term and long-term returns. For example, initial costs for training an AI model might be high, but ongoing benefits from automation can offset them over time.

7.1.3 Gathering Qualitative Insights

Quantitative metrics provide a solid foundation, but qualitative feedback adds valuable context:

- **Employee Feedback**: Conduct focus groups or surveys to understand how employees feel about using generative AI in their workflows. Identify pain points, such as difficulty integrating AI tools, or successes, like increased productivity.

- **Customer Feedback**: Capture customer insights on AI-enhanced services. For instance, survey users about their experiences with AI-generated product recommendations or support interactions.

- **Leadership Perspectives**: Engage executives to evaluate how generative AI aligns with long-term strategic objectives. This feedback can guide adjustments to ensure initiatives remain relevant to business goals.

7.2 Overcoming Challenges in Scaling AI

Scaling generative AI across an organization presents unique challenges. Addressing these challenges effectively is critical for sustained success.

7.2.1 Standardizing Processes

Standardization ensures consistency and scalability across teams and departments:

- **Documentation**: Create detailed process guides for deploying AI models, managing data pipelines, and validating outputs. For example, outline step-by-step procedures for generating and reviewing AI-driven marketing materials.

- **Templates**: Develop templates for common use cases to accelerate implementation. A customer service team, for instance, could use predefined AI chatbot scripts tailored to FAQs.

- **Training Modules**: Provide structured training programs for employees across roles. Include tailored content for technical teams (e.g., model fine-tuning) and non-technical teams (e.g., interpreting AI insights).

7.2.2 Managing Resource Constraints

Scaling AI requires significant resources, but resource constraints can be managed with strategic planning:

- **Cloud Solutions**: Adopt scalable cloud platforms, such as AWS or Google Cloud, to minimize upfront hardware investments while accommodating growing computational needs.

- **Prioritization**: Focus on high-impact projects with clear ROI before expanding AI initiatives. For example, start by automating repetitive tasks in a single department before scaling to others.

- **Internal Talent**: Upskill existing employees to take on AI-related roles. Providing advanced training to technical teams can reduce the need for external hires, saving costs in the long run.

7.2.3 Ensuring Data Consistency and Quality

High-quality, consistent data is the foundation of effective AI systems:

- **Data Governance**: Establish clear policies for data collection, storage, and usage. Ensure compliance with regulations like GDPR or CCPA to protect privacy.

- **Centralized Repositories**: Create a unified data platform to eliminate silos and inconsistencies. For instance, a retail organization might centralize customer purchase data to enhance personalization.

- **Continuous Monitoring**: Implement regular audits of data pipelines to detect and address quality issues. Automated monitoring tools can flag anomalies, ensuring clean data feeds for AI models.

7.2.4 Addressing Organizational Resistance

Resistance to AI adoption can stem from fear of job displacement or lack of understanding:

- **Showcasing Early Wins**: Share success stories from pilot projects to demonstrate the tangible benefits of AI. Highlight metrics like cost savings, efficiency gains, or improved customer satisfaction.

- **Stakeholder Engagement**: Involve employees and leaders early in the process. Soliciting their input and addressing concerns fosters a sense of ownership and reduces resistance.

- **Clear Communication**: Regularly communicate the value of AI initiatives, emphasizing how they enhance rather than replace human roles. For instance, position AI as a tool that automates mundane tasks, freeing employees to focus on strategic activities.

7.3 Building a Roadmap for Scaling Generative AI

A structured roadmap provides clarity and direction for scaling generative AI. Key components include:

7.3.1 Phase-Based Expansion
Scaling AI should follow a phased approach to manage risks and refine strategies:

- **Phase 1: Pilot Projects**: Begin with small-scale pilots to validate feasibility and effectiveness. For instance, implement an AI-driven content generation tool in the marketing team to test its impact.

- **Phase 2: Departmental Scaling**: Expand successful pilots to similar departments or use cases. For example, extend AI-powered chatbots from customer support to HR for handling employee queries.

- **Phase 3: Enterprise-Wide Integration**: Roll out AI initiatives across the entire organization, ensuring interoperability between systems and alignment with overall business objectives.

7.3.2 Cross-Functional Collaboration
Collaboration between departments ensures smooth scaling:

- **Centers of Excellence**: Establish cross-functional teams to oversee AI projects, share best practices, and address challenges. For example, a center of excellence might standardize AI tools across marketing, sales, and operations.

- **Communication Tools**: Use platforms like Slack or Microsoft Teams to facilitate communication and knowledge sharing among AI teams.

7.3.3 Continuous Improvement

Scaling AI is an iterative process requiring ongoing refinement:

- **Feedback Loops**: Collect input from users and stakeholders regularly to identify areas for improvement.

- **Model Updates**: Retrain AI models periodically with new data to maintain accuracy and relevance. For example, update recommendation engines with the latest customer behavior trends.

- **Performance Monitoring**: Use analytics dashboards to track KPIs and identify bottlenecks in AI workflows.

7.4 Case Studies of Successful Scaling

7.4.1 Amazon's Use of AI for Personalization

Amazon has scaled generative AI to provide personalized recommendations, leveraging user behavior data to suggest products. This approach has significantly increased customer satisfaction and driven sales growth.

7.4.2 Coca-Cola's AI-Powered Marketing Campaigns

Coca-Cola employs generative AI to create personalized

marketing materials, such as ad copy and visuals. By scaling these capabilities globally, the company has achieved higher engagement rates and optimized campaign performance.

7.4.3 NVIDIA's Enterprise AI Solutions

NVIDIA's generative AI models support diverse industries, from healthcare to gaming. By scaling their solutions, they enable customers to create realistic simulations, accelerating innovation and reducing costs.

7.5 The Future of Generative AI Scaling

Emerging trends in generative AI will shape future scaling opportunities:

- **Multimodal AI**: Expanding AI systems to handle multiple data types (e.g., text, images, video) enables richer and more versatile applications.

- **Edge AI**: Deploying AI on edge devices, such as smartphones and IoT devices, facilitates real-time processing with lower latency.

- **Sustainable AI**: Innovations in energy-efficient algorithms and hardware reduce the environmental impact of scaling AI systems.

Conclusion

Measuring the impact and scaling generative AI initiatives are critical steps for maximizing their value. By establishing clear metrics, addressing challenges, and building a phased roadmap, organizations can expand AI's reach while maintaining consistency and quality. The next and final chapter will summarize the key insights from this book and provide actionable steps for leveraging generative AI to drive digital transformation.

Chapter 8: Conclusion: Embracing the Future with Generative AI

Generative AI is not just a technological advancement; it is a transformative force that has the potential to redefine how businesses operate, innovate, and grow. Throughout this book, we have explored the foundational concepts of generative AI, its strategic implementation, risk management, workforce transformation, and scaling across an organization. This concluding chapter distills the key insights and provides actionable steps to help organizations fully embrace the opportunities generative AI presents while navigating the challenges it brings.

8.1 Key Takeaways from the Book

8.1.1 Understanding the Foundations

Generative AI, powered by technologies like GPT, GANs, and diffusion models, stands apart from traditional AI by creating new content, designs, and solutions. This capability enables businesses to achieve unprecedented levels of creativity and innovation. For example, AI can generate marketing campaigns, prototype product designs, or synthesize data-driven insights, all of which save time and resources while improving outcomes.

8.1.2 Building a Business Case

To harness generative AI effectively, organizations must focus on aligning AI initiatives with strategic goals. High-impact use cases, such as personalized customer experiences or process automation, provide tangible ROI. The business case becomes stronger when success stories from industries like healthcare, retail, and finance demonstrate the value of adopting generative AI.

8.1.3 Developing a Strategy

A successful strategy requires detailed planning. Organizations must:

- Clearly define objectives for AI initiatives.

- Choose the right tools and platforms.

- Engage stakeholders to ensure alignment with broader business goals. A roadmap outlining pilot projects, departmental scaling, and eventual enterprise-wide adoption is essential for sustainable success.

8.1.4 Managing Risks

Generative AI presents risks such as ethical concerns, data privacy issues, and operational challenges. These risks can be mitigated through governance frameworks, bias audits, and transparency initiatives. Companies must also address the potential misuse of AI, such as creating deepfakes or generating misleading content, by establishing ethical guidelines and content controls.

8.1.5 Upskilling the Workforce

AI adoption is most effective when employees are empowered to work alongside the technology. Upskilling programs that focus on AI literacy, data analysis, and creative problem-solving help employees integrate AI into their workflows. A culture of innovation, supported by leadership and cross-functional collaboration, ensures widespread adoption and impact.

8.1.6 Measuring and Scaling

Measuring the impact of generative AI involves tracking KPIs like efficiency gains, revenue growth, and customer satisfaction. Scaling successful initiatives requires phased implementation, standardized processes, and continuous improvement. By iterating on feedback and refining strategies, organizations can ensure that AI delivers consistent value as it scales.

8.2 Actionable Steps for Organizations

8.2.1 Start Small and Scale Strategically

- **Pilot Projects**: Begin with focused projects that address specific challenges. For example, a retailer might use generative AI to automate product descriptions or enhance personalized recommendations.

- **Iterative Scaling**: Analyze results, gather feedback, and refine processes before expanding to other departments or regions. Use lessons learned from early initiatives to guide broader rollouts.

8.2.2 Invest in Data and Infrastructure

- **Data Quality**: Ensure that training datasets are diverse, accurate, and representative of the business environment. Poor data quality can lead to biased or irrelevant AI outputs.

- **Infrastructure Scalability**: Invest in cloud computing platforms, edge devices, and robust storage solutions to handle the computational demands of generative AI.

Scalable infrastructure ensures that systems can grow alongside organizational needs.

8.2.3 Prioritize Ethics and Transparency

- **Ethical Frameworks**: Develop and enforce guidelines to ensure AI use aligns with company values and societal norms. For example, prohibit the use of AI for generating harmful or misleading content.

- **Transparency Initiatives**: Clearly communicate the role of AI in products and services. Label AI-generated outputs and provide users with the ability to verify their authenticity.

8.2.4 Empower Employees

- **Ongoing Training**: Offer workshops, certifications, and e-learning resources to help employees develop AI-related skills. Ensure programs are tailored to different roles, from technical staff to non-technical teams.

- **Cross-Functional Collaboration**: Encourage collaboration between departments to share knowledge and best practices. For instance, marketing teams might work with data scientists to refine AI-generated campaigns.

8.2.5 Monitor and Adapt

- **Performance Metrics**: Continuously track KPIs to assess the success of AI initiatives. Examples include reduced production times, increased sales, or improved customer retention rates.

- **Iterative Updates**: Adapt AI strategies based on evolving business goals and technological advancements. Regular updates to AI models and processes ensure long-term relevance and effectiveness.

8.3 Looking Ahead: The Future of Generative AI

The future of generative AI holds exciting possibilities, with key trends likely to shape its evolution:

- **Multimodal AI**: The integration of text, images, video, and other data types into a single AI system will enable richer and more versatile applications. For instance, businesses might develop tools that simultaneously generate marketing copy, product visuals, and promotional videos.

- **Hyper-Personalization**: Advances in AI will allow organizations to deliver highly personalized experiences at scale. Examples include tailoring healthcare plans to individual patients or creating custom travel itineraries based on user preferences.

- **Sustainable AI**: With growing concerns about environmental impact, the development of energy-efficient AI models and infrastructure will become a priority. Organizations that adopt sustainable practices can reduce costs while aligning with societal expectations.

- **Ethical Development**: Ensuring responsible AI use will remain critical. Businesses, governments, and researchers must collaborate to establish standards and regulations that promote fairness, accountability, and inclusivity.

Generative AI is poised to drive innovation across industries, but its adoption must be guided by deliberate and thoughtful strategies. Companies that proactively address its challenges while embracing its potential will gain a significant competitive edge.

Conclusion

Generative AI represents a paradigm shift, offering businesses unparalleled opportunities to innovate and grow. By understanding its foundations, managing its risks, empowering the workforce, and scaling strategically, organizations can harness the transformative power of generative AI to achieve sustainable success. The journey may be complex, but the rewards—increased efficiency, creativity, and competitiveness—make it a journey worth undertaking.